HAL LEONARD

PLAYBACK+
Speed • Pitch • Balance • Loop

OUD METHOD
BY JOHN BILEZIKJIAN

Cover photo is of a 1900 Manol Oud, part of the John Bilezikjian oud collection.

All photos by Neil Zlozower, Terry Whitley, and Don Hagopian.

To access audio visit:
www.halleonard.com/mylibrary

2859-1617-5723-0862

ISBN 978-0-634-07786-9

HAL•LEONARD®
7777 W. BLUEMOUND RD. P.O. BOX 13819 MILWAUKEE, WI 53213

In Australia contact:
Hal Leonard Australia Pty. Ltd.
4 Lentara Court
Cheltenham, Victoria, 3192 Australia
Email: ausadmin@halleonard.com

Visit Hal Leonard Online at **www.halleonard.com**

INTRODUCTION

The purpose of this book and its accompanying audio is to give the student not only a method from which to learn the oud, but also an overview of the history, folklore, and origin of this ancient stringed instrument. This book teaches the fundamentals of standard Western music notation in the context of oud playing and serves as an introduction for absolute beginners as well as those experienced on another instrument.

The oud, which literally means "the wood," dates back some 2,500 years and is widely considered the most important instrument to come from the Middle East. It is the predecessor of the European Renaissance-style lute and, ultimately, the guitar. It is also one of the first of the family of all instruments classified as *lutes*—i.e., plucked instruments with strings and a neck. From the prototypes of instruments such as the oud, different lute instruments developed all over the world. The oud has a rich, full acoustic sound, thanks mostly to its large teardrop-shaped body and round back. Standard music notation for the oud is written in treble clef and sounds an octave lower than written (just like the guitar).

There are two types of ouds in use at present, both handmade by luthiers in the Middle East. One is the Turkish variety, which is small compared to its Arabic counterpart. The Turkish oud generally has superior woods and materials, as well as better craftsmanship in its construction than the Arabic variety of instrument.

The oud is commonly played using Middle Eastern *quarter tones* (or *microtones*), subdivisions of the diatonic scale that are not found in most Western music. This takes great skill and practice in its execution as to correct finger placement on the neck of the instrument. Many musicians play the oud in a diatonic fashion, ignoring the quarter tones and replacing them with pitches of a diatonic nature. The traditional system of quarter tones, used centuries ago and to this day in the Middle East, is called *Makam*. For the purposes of this introductory method book, we will not enter into the subject of Makam.

This oud method is written with the right-handed student in mind. If you are left-handed, simply reverse the strings of the oud so that the first course is string number six (single), then re-string appropriately. Likewise, consider all other left and right directional references in reverse. For information on stringing your oud, see the Appendix on page 40.

ABOUT THE AUDIO

The accompanying audio with this book contains 27 tracks of audio for demonstration and play along. Some tracks contain accompaniment oud or dumbeg (Middle Eastern hand drum). In these cases the main written oud part will be on the right channel only and the accompaniment instrument will be on the left channel so you can adjust the panning to the left and play along with the accompaniment part.

ABOUT THE AUTHOR

"America's Oud Virtuoso," John Bilezikjian (1948-2015) had performed on the oud since 1958 until his death. He has made over thirty CDs, all of which are sold through his web site and company, Dantz Records. John appeared in numerous venues throughout America and abroad, from classical settings with the Los Angeles Philharmonic Orchestra to concert halls in Europe. He wrote and recorded traditional music for the oud, rock 'n' roll, music for belly dancing, and television and motion picture soundtracks. You can hear John on recordings by Placido Domingo, Ofra Haza, Robert Palmer, Cantor Isaac Behar, Leonard Cohen, and many others.

In 1967, John was one of the pioneers in electrifying the oud with a DeArmond pickup. In 1969 he was the first to use a Barcus-Berry transducer placed under the face of the oud. At the time, it was considered a terrible risk to place a sound device inside the instrument; it would require taking out the center rosette and drilling a 1/4" hole in the butt end of the oud. No player had thought of doing such a thing, but in John's case it worked so well that others decided to try the idea as well. In 1969, Mikhael Kollander and John Bilezikjian developed a flat-back version of the oud; it too was electrified with a transducer. Imitations of their original design have appeared in the last few years through other makers.

For more information on John Bilezikjian and the oud, see **www.dantzrecords.com**.

THE OUD

HOW TO FIND AN OUD

Concerning those students who find that they may need to purchase an oud and/or accessories for the oud, such as oud strings and oud picks (called *mzraps*), please visit **www.dantzrecords.com**.

This book is designed for use with the standard oud of Turkish or Arabic design; both have eleven strings, arranged as one single string and five courses of two strings in unison. You will not find any frets (or bars) on the neck of the oud, as you would on a guitar or most similar instruments.

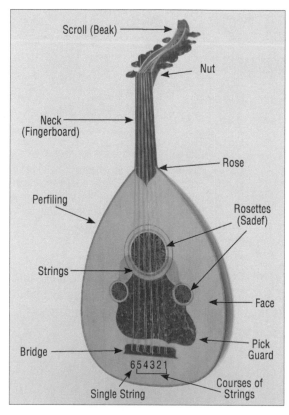

Turkish Oud front
(1968 Onnik Karibyan Oud made in Istanbul, Turkey)

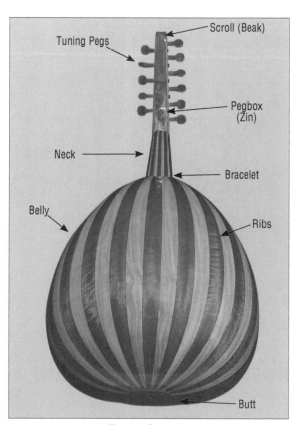

Turkish Oud belly
(2004 Mustapha Cupçuoglu Oud made in Istanbul, Turkey)

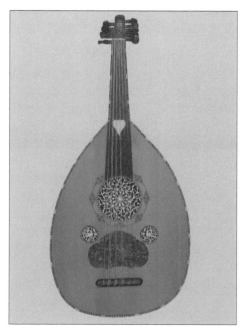

Arabic Oud
(1939 Dicran Najarian Oud made in Aleppo, Syria)

TUNING

There are many tunings for the oud, and players are experimenting all the time. For the purposes of this method, we will use the Turkish/Armenian tuning, which is most commonly used today. The pitches, from low to high, are E–A–B–E–A–D.

Another popular tuning is the Arabic tuning (low to high): D–G–A–D–G–C. This is one whole step below the Turkish/Armenian tuning.

There are many different ways to get your oud in tune. First, if you are using the oud method book/audio package, listen to track 1. You will hear guide tones that match the pitches of the open oud strings in Turkish/Armenian tuning, from low to high.

You can also tune to a piano or an electronic keyboard (the piano should be in tune). Play the correct key (see diagram) for each open string, and match your oud strings to that.

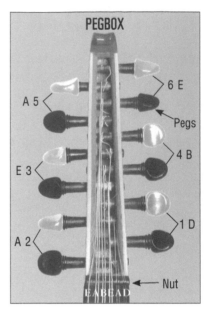

The darkened peg is the string on the right of the pair of strings as you are holding the oud vertically and facing you. Notice there are 12 pegs and only 11 strings. Some players choose to add another string.

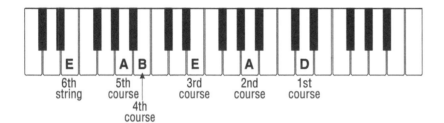

You can also use an electronic tuner, which can be purchased at any music store that sells musical accessories. An electronic tuner is a good way to get accurately in tune until your ear is trained to hear pitches. There are many different kinds available; just make sure the tuner you use has a built-in microphone that can pick up the pitches of an acoustic instrument.

HOW TO TUNE YOUR OUD

TRACK 1

Hold the oud in front of you, either vertically with the butt end touching the floor, or horizontally in playing position. Find the tuning peg that controls the string you want to tune, and slowly turn the peg until it matches the note you are tuning to.

Start with the second course of strings, for which the pitch is A. Tune both strings to match an A note, matching up the open string with whatever source note you use (audio track, keyboard, or electronic tuner). Make sure that both strings sound the same note when played together.

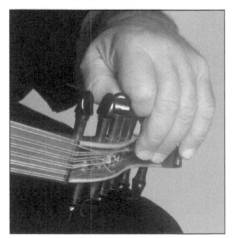

Horizontal Tuning Position

Continue this process for all the strings, matching each open string or course to its respective note (low to high): E–A–B–E–A–D. You will find that you have to repeat this procedure several times, because ouds have friction pegs that tend to slip from time to time. At first, it may take several attempts to complete the tuning process and you should recheck your tuning often. Slipping pegs are common in all ouds. By trial and error, the student will find the best way to overcome the problem. Make sure that once a string is in tune, the peg is pushed firmly into the hole in which it sits. Also, chalk or peg dope helps to keep pegs from slipping.

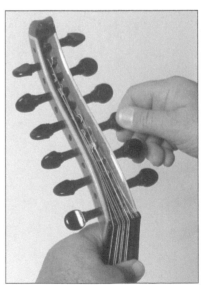

Vertical Tuning Position

PLAYING POSITION

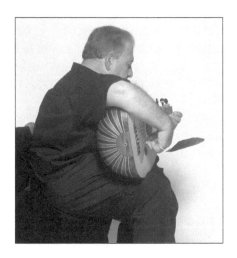

The oud is traditionally played in a seated position, similar to that of a guitar. Rest the oud on your right thigh and hold it parallel to the ground. Hold the instrument against your body, just as you would a guitar. Since the oud has a rounded back, it is important to find a comfortable holding position that keeps it upright. An optional footstool under the right foot often helps keep the oud at a playable level and reduces back strain. The need for a footstool may depend on your height or the height of your chair.

THE LEFT HAND

Fingers of the left hand are numbered 1 through 4.

Place the thumb in back of the neck, directly behind where the fingers touch the fingerboard. Try to keep a pencil diameter's distance of room between the back of the fingerboard and your left palm.

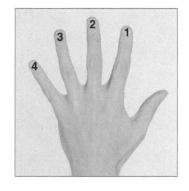

THE RIGHT HAND

Whereas a guitar is commonly played with a pick, the oud is played with a different kind of plectrum called a *mzrap* (Turkish) or *resha* (Arabic). The traditional plectrum is an eagle's quill. In the twentieth century a new plectrum, made of plastic and Teflon, was introduced. This is the most common plectrum in use today, though the eagle's quill is sometimes still used.

Teflon Pick   Eagle's Feather Quill

In sitting position, the plectrum is held in the right hand, between the index finger and thumb, so that approximately 1/4" of the pick sticks out. The wrist is held at a 90° angle to the strings in playing position.

MUSIC NOTATION

The Western musical language is based on the first seven letters of the English alphabet: A–B–C–D–E–F–G. Each letter corresponds to a note. Music has notes that are low and high; when a player plays notes that cover an eight-note interval, in any order, this is referred to as an **octave**. Playing beyond these eight notes creates another octave. The oud has up to three playable octaves, although most players perform within two octaves.

Musical notes are written along five horizontal lines, known as a **staff**. Where a note is positioned on the staff determines its **pitch** (highness or lowness). Our musical system identifies these five lines with a **clef sign**. Different clefs are used for different instruments. For the oud, we use the **treble clef**.

The five notes that fall on the lines of the staff are (low to high) E–G–B–D–F. You can remember these as "Every Good Boy Does Fine." The spaces are (low to high) F–A–C–E.

A **measure** (also known as a "bar") is the space between two **bar lines**. A **final bar** ends a piece of music.

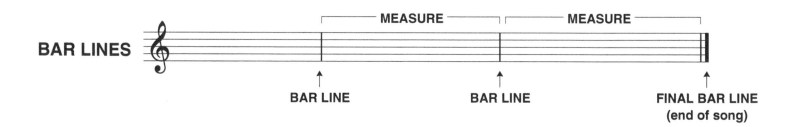

Each measure contains a specific number of **beats**, determined by the **rhythm** of the composition. The rhythm is shown by the **time signature** at the beginning of the piece of music (next to the clef). One of the basic time signatures is 4/4, in which there are four beats in a measure and a quarter note gets one beat.

RHYTHM VALUES

Notes indicate the **pitch** and **duration** of a musical tone (how long it lasts within a measure). There are different kinds of notes to indicate different durations:

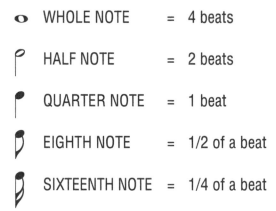

o	WHOLE NOTE	= 4 beats
	HALF NOTE	= 2 beats
	QUARTER NOTE	= 1 beat
	EIGHTH NOTE	= 1/2 of a beat
	SIXTEENTH NOTE	= 1/4 of a beat

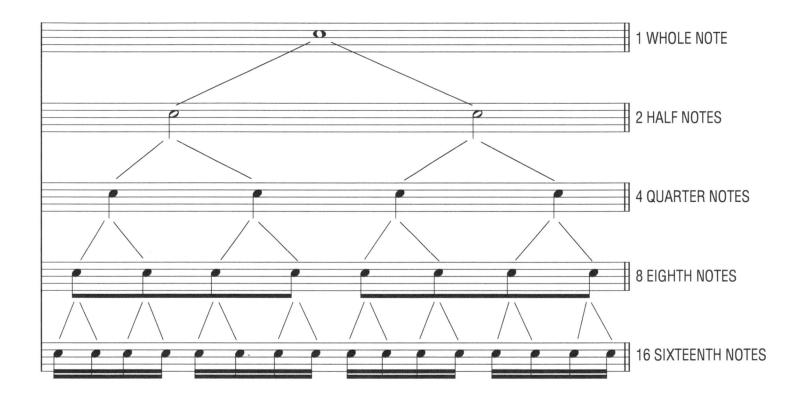

1 WHOLE NOTE

2 HALF NOTES

4 QUARTER NOTES

8 EIGHTH NOTES

16 SIXTEENTH NOTES

RESTS

Rests indicate moments of silence. The most common rests correspond to the notes above.

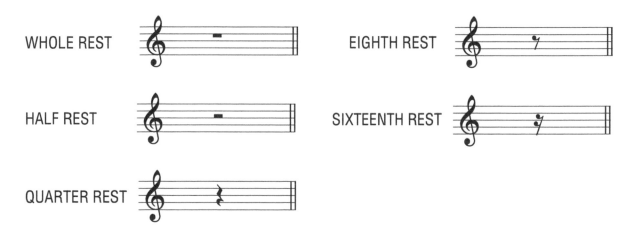

WHOLE REST

HALF REST

QUARTER REST

EIGHTH REST

SIXTEENTH REST

OPEN STRINGS

"Open-String: Study #1" begins on the open low E string, a note that is too low for the staff. Notes like this are written with **ledger lines**—extended staff lines that allow for lower and higher notes. Consider them an extension of the musical staff.

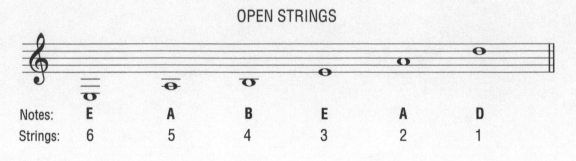

PICKING

This sign (⊓) tells you to strike the strings with a downward motion of the mzrap, or a **downstroke**.

Try playing the example first with all downstrokes, then alternating downstrokes and **upstrokes** (∨). Do this slowly and try to maintain a steady rhythm throughout. Always start and stop on a downstroke.

The zeros shown in the notation indicate that the notes to be played are open strings and not fingered.

OPEN-STRING: STUDY #1

TRACK 2

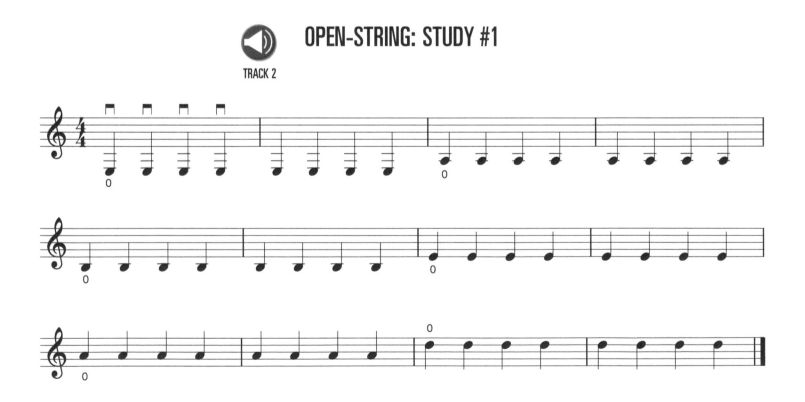

THE FINGERBOARD

This diagram shows six **positions** on the fingerboard of the oud, as well as the ½ position closest to the nut, and the fingering that corresponds to each. These positions will be referred to throughout this book, so look back at this chart often. It also shows where the notes are on each string. The sixth position is where your left hand meets the body of the oud. Roman numerals are used throughout the book to indicate fingerboard positions.

The diagram also introduces **sharps** (♯) and **flats** (♭), also known as **accidentals**. F♯ is the note between F and G; B♭ is the note between A and B. A **natural sign** (♮) next to a note cancels out a previous sharp or flat. You will learn more about accidentals as you progress.

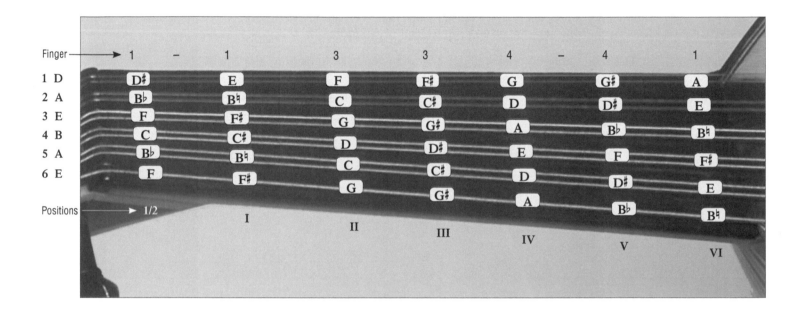

SHIFTING POSITIONS

Notice that when you move from one position to the next, your entire hand will shift. Try playing the ½-position F note on string 6 with your first finger. Then play the F♯ note in first position on the same string with the first finger; your hand shifts up the fingerboard, so you are now in the next position.

FINGERBOARD TIPS

For help finding the positions along the oud neck, put a small piece of colored tape along the edge of the entire fingerboard showing positions ½ through 6. This will help you play in tune by showing where to put your fingers on the fingerboard.

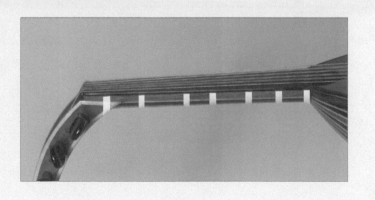

SCALES

THE CHROMATIC SCALE

Chromatic notes are tones that are one half step apart from one another. The **chromatic scale** is extremely important in the study of the oud—in fact, it is the bible for oud players. It will show you where all of the notes and their fingerings are.

The examples below are shown on four different levels:

1. The numbers above the staff tell you what string (or course of strings) to play.

2. The staff notation tells you what note to play.

3. The numbers under the notes tell you which left-hand finger to use to play the note ("o" indicates an open string; "–" tells you to slide the indicated finger up or down to the next note).

4. The Roman numerals on the bottom tell you what position you need to be in to play the notes.

The first example begins in first position. Start on the sixth string for the first five notes, then move on accordingly. When you know where to find the notes, play along with track 3 and try to match what is played on the track. This may take some time since you have no frets to guide you, but the note positions will become intuitive after some practice.

TRACK 3

Ascending Chromatic Scale

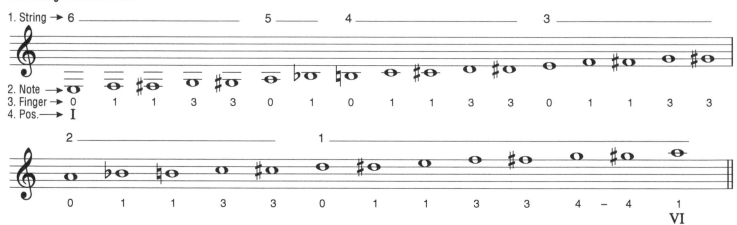

Descending Chromatic Scale

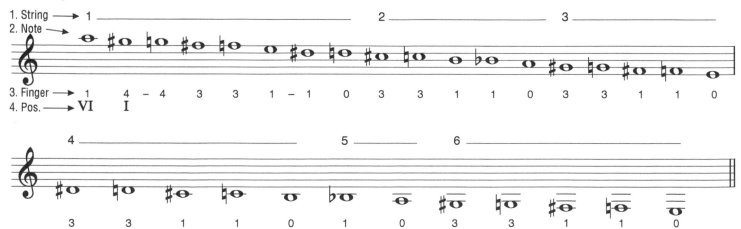

MAJOR SCALES

The examples below show the fingerings of the **major scales**, one of the basic building blocks of melody in music. Learning these scales, and the minor scales that follow, will give you a foundation for playing all kinds of music on the oud.

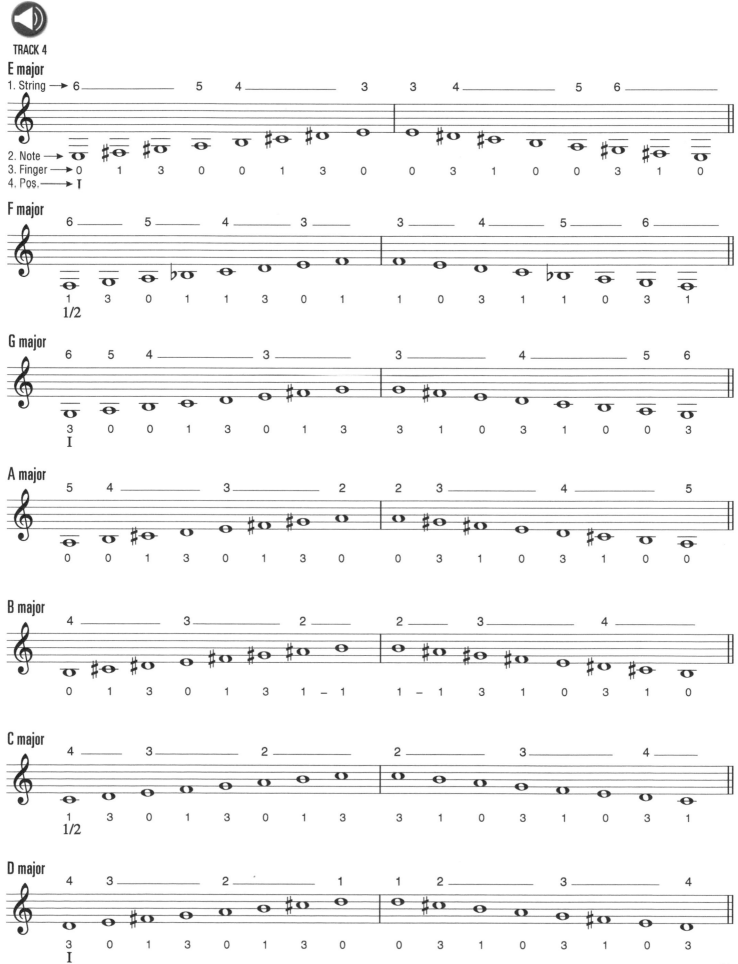

MINOR SCALES

The **minor scale** is equally important as a melodic foundation. It has a slightly darker, sadder sound than its major counterpart. There are several different types of minor scales, but here you will learn **harmonic minor,** a scale common to Middle Eastern music. The primary harmonic minor scales and their fingerings are shown below.

TRACK 5

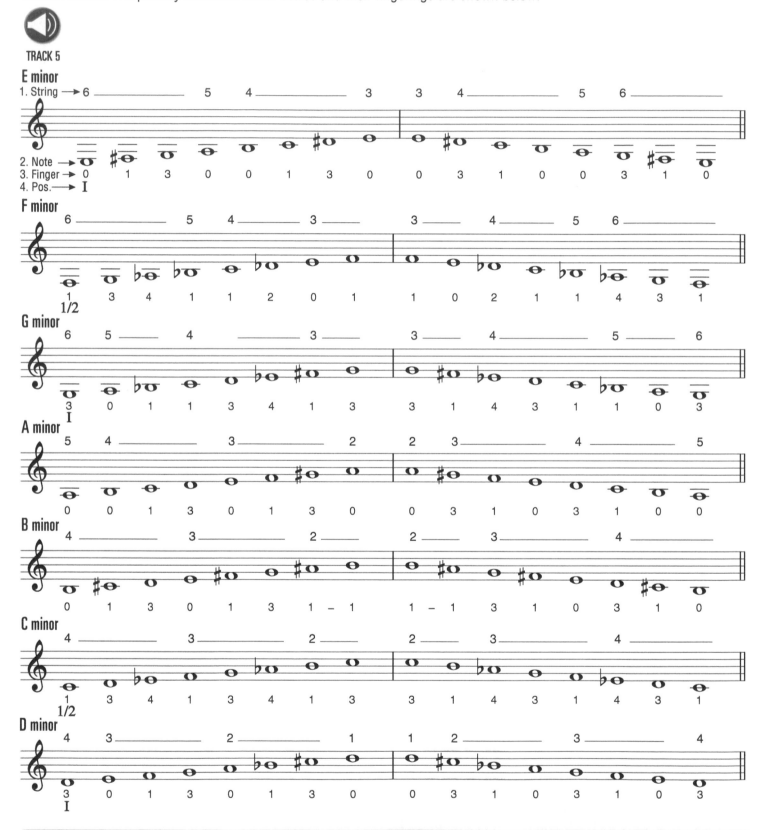

ENHARMONIC EQUIVALENTS

Notice that the Ab in the F minor scale is the same note as the G# in the E major scale. These are called **enharmonic equivalents,** and you will see them often. Whether a note is called sharp or flat depends on what key you are playing in, and often what direction (higher or lower) you are coming from.

KEY SIGNATURES

Instead of writing a sharp sign before every F in a song, one sharp sign is placed at the beginning of each line of the song. This is called a key signature and indicates that every F in the song (high or low) should be played as F#. In "Little Oud: Study #2" there will be an arrow above the staff every time this happens.

 LITTLE OUD: STUDY #2

TRACK 6

John Bilezikjian

Study #3 has four sharps in the key signature: F, C, G, and D. This tells us that it is in the key of E, and most of its notes come from the E major scale.

STUDY #3

TRACK 7

John Bilezikjian

EIGHTH NOTES

An **eighth note** is half the length of a quarter note and receives half a beat in 4/4 or 3/4 meter.

One eighth note is written with a flag. Consecutive eighth notes are connected with a beam.

To count eighth notes, divide the beat into two, and use "and" between the beats. Count the measure to the right aloud while tapping your foot on the beat.

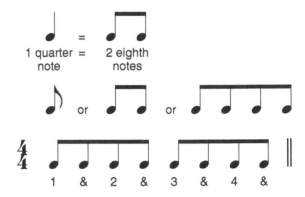

Exercise #1 introduces eighth notes. Wherever they occur, try to play them with even up and downstrokes.

EXERCISE #1: A MINOR

TRACK 8

John Bilezikjian

Now play the previous exercise in the key of E minor.

TRACK 9

EXERCISE #2: E MINOR

John Bilezikjian

TREMOLO PICKING

A double line across the stem of a note (♩) means that it is to be played with tremolo (in rapid down and upstrokes) for its duration. Begin each tremolo note with a downstroke, and try to play all strokes evenly.

TREMOLO: STUDY #4

TRACK 10

John Bilezikjian

REVIEW

These next few songs combine all of the elements you have learned so far with some new concepts.

THE RITARD

The **ritard** symbol (*rit.*) at the end of "Hatikvah" tells you to slow down gradually until the end of the tune.

HATIKVAH

TRACK 11

National Anthem of Israel
Arr. by John Bilezikjian

FLATS AND SHARPS

TRACK 12

John Bilezikjian

A **dot** after a note makes it 1½ times longer than usual; a **dotted half note** (♩.) takes up three beats, and a **dotted quarter note** (♩.) takes up one and a half beats.

 ## MORE FLATS AND SHARPS

TRACK 13

John Bilezikjian

RHYTHMS AND METERS

3/4 TIME

"My First Song" is in **3/4 time**: there are three beats per measure, and a quarter note gets one beat.

MY FIRST SONG

TRACK 14

John Bilezikjian

6/8 TIME AND REPEATS

In **6/8 time**, there are six beats to a measure, and an eighth note gets one beat.

Repeat signs tell you to repeat everything that is between them. Play through the section once until you hit the second repeat sign (:‖), then go back to the first repeat sign (‖:), play the section again, and continue to the end.

6/8

TRACK 15

John Bilezikjian

2/4 TIME

In **2/4 time**, there are two beats per measure, and a quarter note gets one beat. Treat it like 4/4 time cut in half.

DOTTED EIGHTH AND SIXTEENTH NOTES

Like the other dotted notes you've played, the dot after an eighth note increases the value of the note by one-half. Since the **dotted eighth note** receives only a part of a beat in 4/4, 3/4, or 2/4 time, a sixteenth is added to it to complete the beat.

A **sixteenth note** has a stem with either two flags or two beams. It lasts half as long as an eighth note, or one quarter of a beat.

This tune combines dotted eighth notes with sixteenth notes (♪ ♬) for a staggered rhythm. Listen to track 16 to get a feel for these new rhythms.

THE DOTTED NOTE

TRACK 16

John Bilezikjian

This tune combines straight sixteenth notes with eighth and quarter notes. Play the groups of sixteenths with even up and downstrokes.

ORIENTALE DANCE

TRACK 17

John Bilezikjian

EXERCISE #3: EIGHTH NOTES IN 3/4

TRACK 18

John Bilezikjian

RHYTHMS FROM ARMENIA AND THE MIDDLE EAST

Played on **dumbeg** (Middle Eastern hand drum; pronounced "Doom-bek")

TRACK 19

Any serious oud player should get familiar with certain rhythms of the Mediterranean and Middle East, many of which are in **odd time**—the measures are broken up into numbers of beats that may be unfamiliar to the Western ear. Listen to the next track to get familiar with some of these rhythms, then learn the songs that follow.

Kasap (pronounced "Kah-sop")

Turkish/Arabic

*Curcena (pronounced "Jour-jena")

Armenian

Longa

Turkish

Saz Semai (pronounced "Saz Suh-my")

Turkish/Arabic

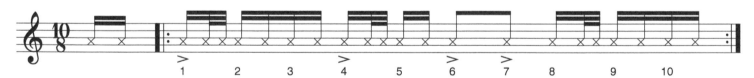

Kalamatiano

Greek

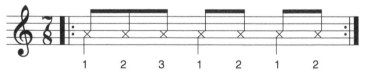

Tsamiko (pronounced "Tsa-mee-ko")

Greek

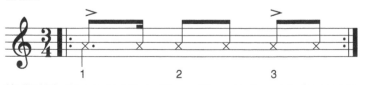

*Karşilama (pronounced "Kar-shi-la-ma")

Turkish

Beledy (pronounced "Bell-leh-dee")

Arabic

Waltz

Laz

Turkish/Greek/Macedonian

Zeybek/Zeybekikko (pronounced "Zay-beh-kee-ko")

Turkish/Greek

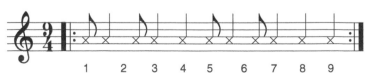

*In Turkish, the c and s letters with a cedilla under them, ç and ş, are pronounced as "ch" and "sh." The letter c is equivalent to the English "j" sound.

SONG IN KASAP RHYTHM

TRACK 20

John Bilezikjian

SONG IN KARŞILAMA RHYTHM

TRACK 21

John Bilezikjian

TIES

Measure 4 in this song includes a note (B) that is **tied** (♩‿♩) over to the next note. Two notes that are tied together become one. Play the first note only, and simply let it ring out (or sustain) for the duration of both notes—then complete the measure.

SONG IN CURCENA RHYTHM

TRACK 22

John Bilezikjian

SONG IN BELEDY RHYTHM

John Bilezikjian

PLAYING CHORDS

A **chord** is created when more than two notes or strings are played at the same time. The oud is not traditionally a chordal instrument, but it can be. Because there are no frets, it is important to listen to the notes you are playing, and make any subtle adjustments to make sure they are on pitch. The chart below shows you all the basic chord positions on the oud and the notes on the staff that make them up.

CHORDS

T = thumb   o = open string   > = one finger over two strings (called a **barre**)

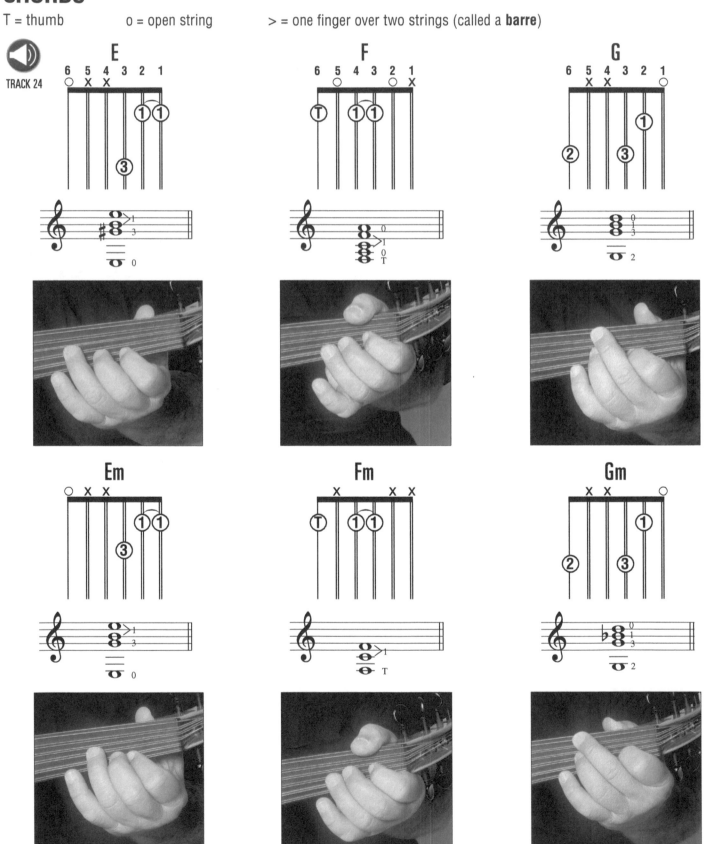

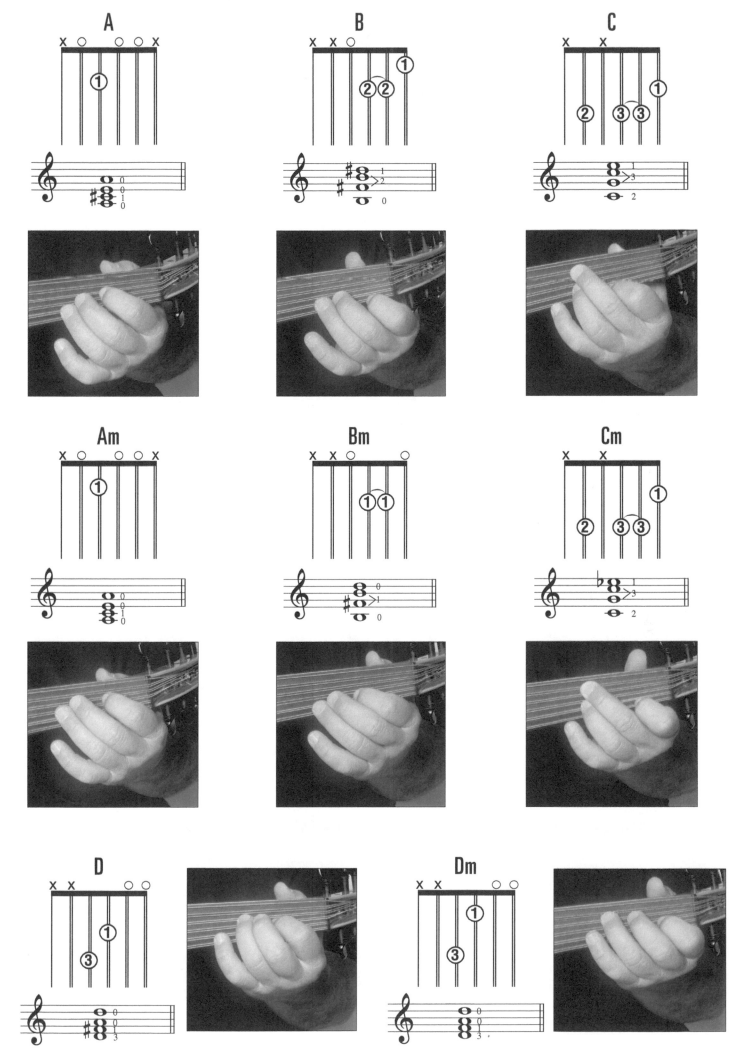

ARPEGGIOS

An **arpeggio** is a group of notes played one-by-one that make up a chord. In the following exercises, each chord tone is played separately to outline or "suggest" the chord.

ARPEGGIOS

TRACK 25

John Bilezikjian

DUET

"Bagatelle" is written for two ouds with complimenting melodies. Try playing through the oud 1 part, then oud 2; they are panned separately (left and right) on the audio, so you can pan out the part you are playing and hear the interaction of your oud with the other. Unless otherwise shown, all notes are to be played with the traditional fingerings learned in this book. At measures 57–64, an easier Oud 1–Alternate part is introduced with eighth notes instead of sixteenth notes. This version is played on track 27.

TRACK 26 TRACK 27 (Easier Version) **BAGATELLE**

John Bilezikjian

*Oud 1 – Alternate is a less difficult option to play for measures 57–64.

37

GLOSSARY

Accidentals: Musical symbols positioned to the left of a note to raise, lower, or return to normal the pitch of the note. *(9)*

Ayub: (pronounced "I-yoob") Arabic name for 4/4 rhythm.

Bar lines: Vertical lines placed on a staff dividing beats into measures. *(6)*

Beat: The basic time unit of a composition (ex: 4/4 time has four beats per measure). *(6)*

Beledy: (pronounced "Bell-leh-dee") Arabic rhythm in 4/4 time. *(24)*

Caprice: Name given to a composition for oud study; (Fr) Whimsical, humorous.

Chords: Three or more tones played simultaneously in harmony. *(28)*

Chromatic Scale: A scale having twelve notes within an octave. *(11)*

Clef: A sign at the beginning of a staff which shows a specific range (e.g. treble clef). *(6)*

Curcena: (pronounced "Jour-jena") Iraqi, Turkish, and Armenian folk rhythm in 10/8. *(24)*

Diatonic: "Two tone" – Musical pitches which are a half step apart from each other; the scale commonly used in Western music. (1)

Downstroke: To strike the strings with a downward motion of the mzrap; notated with (⊓). *(5)*

Dumbeg: (pronounced "Doom-bek") Middle Eastern, hourglass-shaped hand drum with a lambskin or synthetic head and one open end. *(24)*

Eagle's Quill: Traditional plectrum for the oud from ancient times into the present day, though largely replaced by the modern Teflon plectrum. *(5)*

Enharmonic Equivalents: Two identical notes with different letter names (e.g. A♯ and B♭). *(13)*

Exercise: A practice study stressing a technical aspect of a player's musical training.

Filigree: (Rosettes) Fine lace-like designs inside the three holes on the face of the oud. *(3)*

Guido de Arezzo: (995–1025 A.D.) Inventor of the musical staff and modern Western musical notation in the Eleventh Century.

Kalamatiano: Greek rhythm in 7/8. *(24)*

Karşilama: (pronounced "Kar-shi-la-ma") Turkish rhythm in 9/8. *(24)*

Kasap: (pronounced "Kah-sop") Turkish rhythm in 4/4. *(24)*

Key: A scale; the dominant tonality of a piece of music; often the tonic (first) note of a scale. *(13)*

Key Signature: A group of accidentals at the beginning of a staff; shows the performer the key of a piece of music. *(13)*

Laz: Turkish folk rhythm in 7/8. *(24)*

Longa: Turkish march/art rhythm in 2/4. (24)

Makam: A series of pitches that suggests a feeling; the Middle Eastern system of quarter tones. (1)

Major: (Greater) A scale or chord in which the third tone is raised a half step. (11)

Measure: Area on a musical staff between two bar lines; division which contains a certain number of beats. *(6)*

Minor: (Less; Smaller) A scale or chord in which the third tone is lowered a half step. *(11)*

Musical Alphabet: System of music that has seven letter names for notes—A, B, C, D, E, F, and G—referred to as an *octave.* (6)

Mzrap: (Turkish; pronounced "Muz-rahp") Plectrum used for oud playing, held by the right hand to strike the strings (for the right-handed player). *(5)*

Octave: An interval of eight notes. *(6)*

Oud/'Ud: Ancient Persian/Middle Eastern fretless, eleven-stringed lute instrument, dating back some 2500 years, played widely throughout the Middle East. *(1)*

Perfiling: Trim used on the outer edges of the oud and around the three rosettes on the oud face. *(3)*

Positions: Various points on the oud neck where the player's left hand is placed. *(10)*

Repeat Signs: Musical symbols placed on the staff to indicate that a section of music is to be repeated. *(21)*

Resha: (Arabic; pronounced "Ree-sha") See *Mzrap.* (5)

Rest: Musical symbol used to indicate moments of silence in a composition. *(7)*

Rhythm: Consistent pulse in a composition; basic unit of time in a composition (e.g. 4/4). *(6)*

Rose: Arabesque design at the end of the fingerboard where it meets the body of the oud. *(3)*

Scale: A series of notes within the space of an octave that implies a certain tonality. *(10)*

Saz Semai: (pronounced "Saz Suh-my") Turkish art rhythm in 10/8 with accents on beats 1, 4, 6, 7, and 10. *(24)*

Staff: Five horizontal lines on which music is written. *(6)*

Tempo: (Time) Pace (fast or slow) at which a composition is performed.

Time Signature: Pair of numbers at the beginning of a piece of music which indicate the rhythm (i.e. 4/4, 2/4, 3/4, etc.) (6)

Treble Clef: Clef used in writing music for the oud; music written sounds one octave lower. *(8)*

Tremolo: Rapid repetition of a note; fast back-and-forth movement of the plectrum hand which allows a note to sustain. *(15)*

Tsamiko: (pronounced "Tsa-mee-ko") Greek folk rhythm in 3/4. *(24)*

Upstroke: To strike the string with an upward motion of the mzrap; notated with (v). *(5)*

Zeybek: Turkish folk rhythm in 9/4. *(24)*

APPENDIX

HOW TO TIE THE STRINGS TO THE OUD BRIDGE

One way of tying the string to the bridge:

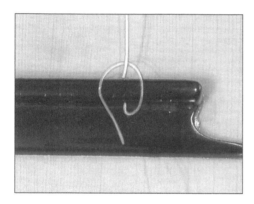 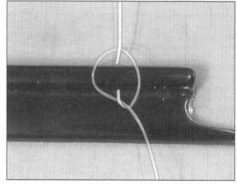 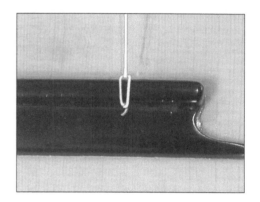

Another way to tie the string to the bridge:

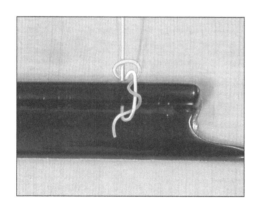 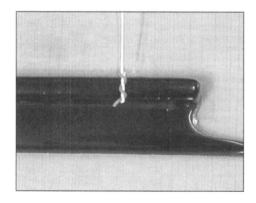

Ultimately, when all the strings are tied on, it will look like this:

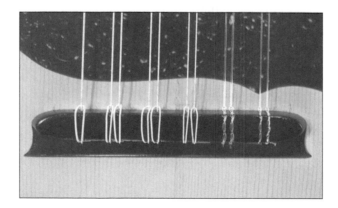